CRUE
CRIME

CONTENTS

Words that look like this are explained in the glossary on page 31.

Photo Credits
Images are courtesy of Shutterstock.com. With thanks to Getty Images, Thinkstock Photo and iStockphoto.
Front Cover – Macrovector, Laborant, ZARIN ANDREY, Tereshchenko Dmitry. 4–5 – javarman, SofiaV, lady–luck, illustrissima. 6–7 – Puslatronik, proslgn, SimpleThings, waewkid. 8–9 – Morphart Creation, guidopiano, Dm_Cherry. 10–11 – Andrey Burmakin, owncham, Kachalkina Veronika, Fun Way Illustration. 12–13 – New Africa, artemiya, witsanu deetuam. 14–15 – Dmitrijs Mihejevs, meunierd, German Vizulis, Krasovski Dmitri. 16–17 – Olha Zinovatna, JIR Moronta, Steve Allen. 18–19 – vectorlab2D, ZARIN ANDREY. 20–21 – Photo-Art-Lortie, Steve Bruckmann, BlueRingMedia. 22–23 – givaga, Luis Louro, Bobby Stevens Photo, Phant, GoodStudio . 24–25 – tynyuk, Sergii Gnatiuk, Marina Datsenko, Sergey Nesterchuk. 26–27 – digitmilk, kittirat roekburi, Zoe Esteban, Raland, Everett Collection. 28–29 – Tiko Aramyan, Krakenimages.com, SHCHERBAKOV SERHII, TheLiftCreativeServices, Tomacco. 30 – Tinnakorn jorruang.

BookLife
PUBLISHING

©2023
BookLife Publishing Ltd.
King's Lynn, Norfolk
PE30 4LS, UK

A catalogue record for this book is available from the British Library.

ISBN: 978-1-80155-845-7

Written by:
William Anthony

Edited by:
Hermione Redshaw

Designed by:
Drue Rintoul

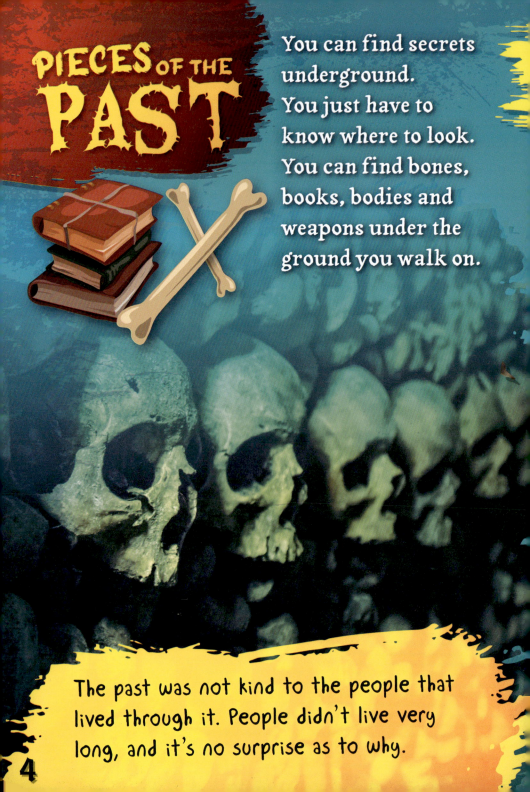

PIECES OF THE PAST

You can find secrets underground. You just have to know where to look. You can find bones, books, bodies and weapons under the ground you walk on.

The past was not kind to the people that lived through it. People didn't live very long, and it's no surprise as to why.

Disease and war were everywhere. People were punished for crimes they did not commit. No one was ever far from disaster, either. Yet, people still lived their lives.

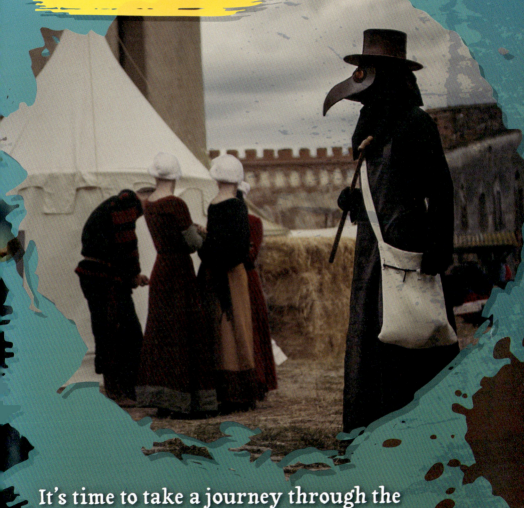

It's time to take a journey through the past. Be prepared for gruesome events and horrible punishments as we enter the hideous history of crime...

PIRATE BUSINESS

Have you ever heard of Blackbeard? What about Barbarossa? You probably think they are some of the most fearsome pirates of all time.

They were nothing compared to Ching Shih. She was one of the greatest pirates of all time. <u>Historians</u> believe she was born in China in 1775.

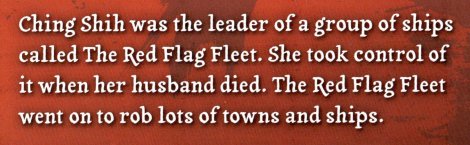

Ching Shih was the leader of a group of ships called The Red Flag Fleet. She took control of it when her husband died. The Red Flag Fleet went on to rob lots of towns and ships.

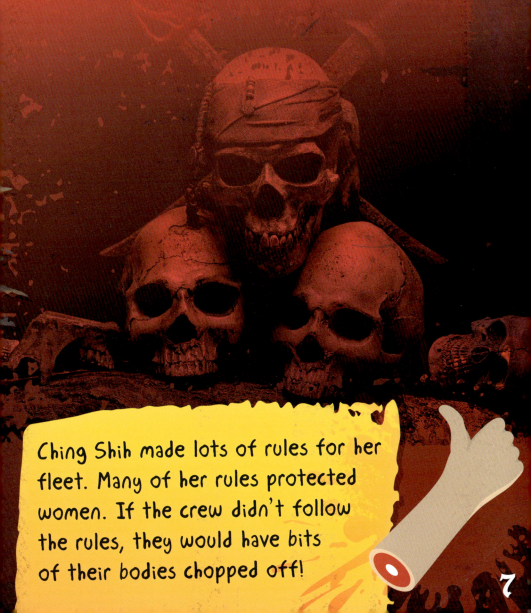

Ching Shih made lots of rules for her fleet. Many of her rules protected women. If the crew didn't follow the rules, they would have bits of their bodies chopped off!

THE UNKNOWN KILLER

In 1888, there was a killer on the loose in London. His name was Jack the Ripper. It is thought that Jack killed five or six people.

Jack the Ripper was never caught. His crimes were so famous that some people are still trying to solve them today!

We know for sure that the Ripper killed five women. He chopped up their bodies with a long, sharp knife in the middle of the night. The police thought he might have been a butcher or a doctor.

yours truly
Jack the Ripper

Lots of letters were sent to the police claiming to be from Jack the Ripper. Historians think these letters were just tricks.

STEALING FROM THE RICH

Robin Hood was an <u>outlaw</u> in England around the 12th <u>century</u>. He knew how to fight with a bow and arrow. He lived in Sherwood Forest with other outlaws called the Merry Men.

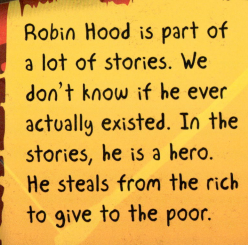

Robin Hood is part of a lot of stories. We don't know if he ever actually existed. In the stories, he is a hero. He steals from the rich to give to the poor.

Records show that outlaws often called themselves names that sounded like Robin Hood. People think this might be because of the story. Others think it is because he really existed.

If Robin Hood and the Merry Men did exist, they were probably more violent than in the stories. In some stories, the Merry Men killed someone. That's not heroic!

THE SCENE OF THE CRIME

There was once a real-life version of Sherlock Holmes in France. His name was Edmund Locard. He changed the way people <u>investigated</u> crimes.

Locard solved crimes with science. He used clues instead of <u>witnesses</u>.

He spent lots of time <u>researching</u> fingerprints. He worked out that if someone left fingerprints at a crime scene, police could find the criminal.

Locard also worked out that things such as makeup and hairs can be passed between two people when they touch.

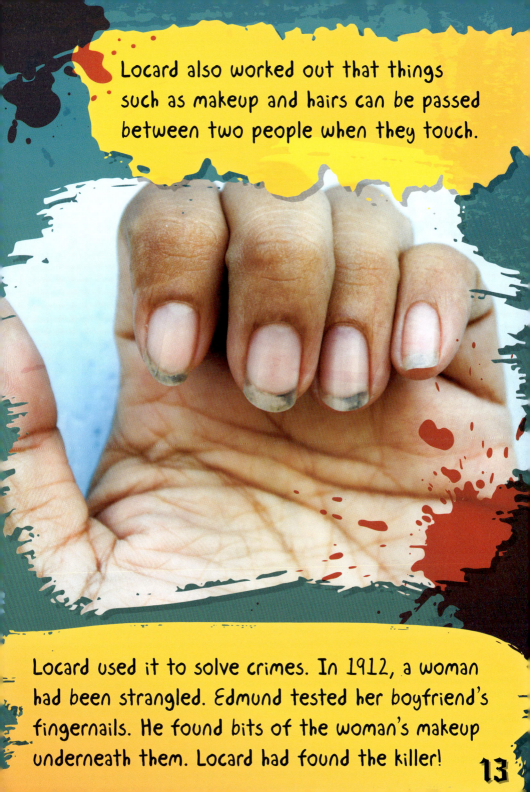

Locard used it to solve crimes. In 1912, a woman had been strangled. Edmund tested her boyfriend's fingernails. He found bits of the woman's makeup underneath them. Locard had found the killer!

THE WILD, WILD WEST

In the late parts of the 19th century, the western parts of North America became known for crime. Many people ignored the <u>law</u> and did lots of bad things.

Police had guns. Outlaws had guns. Ordinary people had guns. It was no wonder there were lots of gunfights in the Wild West!

A famous group of outlaws were called the Wild Bunch. They were led by Butch Cassidy. They made money by robbing trains and banks.

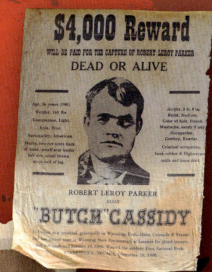

$4,000 Reward

WILL BE PAID FOR THE CAPTURE OF ROBERT LEROY PARKER

DEAD OR ALIVE

ROBERT LEROY PARKER
ALIAS
"BUTCH" CASSIDY

Billy the Kid was one of the most well-known gunmen in the Wild West. He was once captured by police, but he escaped and went on the run. He was finally caught and shot.

REMEMBER, REMEMBER

One of the most famous criminals in Britain's history didn't even get the chance to commit his crime. He was called Guy Fawkes.

NOV
5

He planned to blow up the Houses of Parliament in London. His criminal group tried to put gunpowder underneath the building on the 5th of November in 1605. This became known as the Gunpowder Plot.

However, someone caused the plan to fail. They sent a letter to the government and Royal Family about the plan. Guy Fawkes was arrested, taken away and killed in a gruesome way!

The Gunpowder Plot is remembered every year on the 5th of November in Britain. People light big fires and set off fireworks.

BIG EARS

Lots of people thought the answer to crime was simple. If you broke the law, you got punished in a pretty awful way.

In the 19th century, some people tried to understand the link between crimes and criminals. Were some people more likely to be criminals than others? If so, maybe crimes could be stopped before they happened!

A man called Cesare Lombroso studied criminals. Lombroso thought there was a certain type of person who broke the law. He said most criminals had messy teeth, wonky faces and big ears!

CESARE LOMBROSO

Lombroso was wrong. Nobody is born a criminal just because of how they look. It turns out that you can't just arrest someone for having big ears!

ON THE RUN

Bonnie and Clyde met in 1930 and fell in love. Clyde was arrested for burglary soon after. Bonnie visited him in prison every day and even sneaked a gun into prison to help him escape.

Bonnie and Clyde ran away together. For two years, the couple joined gangs to rob banks. They killed anyone who got in their way.

Life on the run isn't as exciting as it might sound. Bonnie and Clyde took baths in rivers and ate food from cans. They were always on the lookout to make sure they weren't caught.

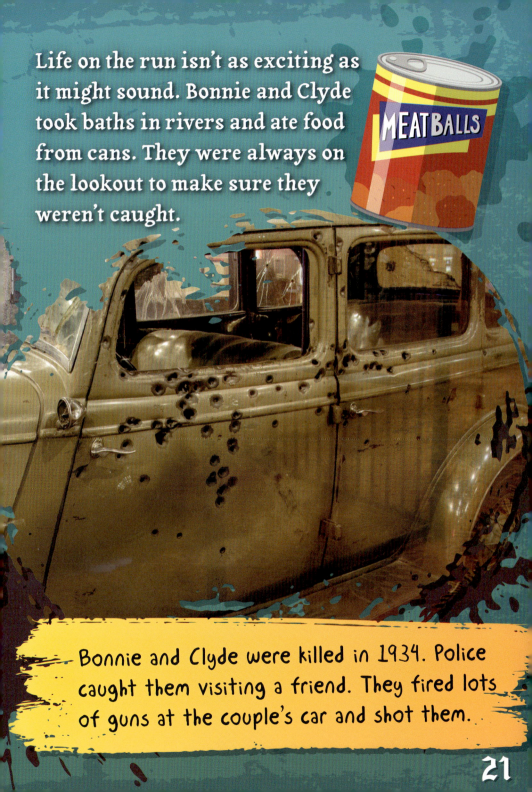

MEATBALLS

Bonnie and Clyde were killed in 1934. Police caught them visiting a friend. They fired lots of guns at the couple's car and shot them.

ROMAN RULES

Ancient Rome was not the nicest place. Wee and poo rained down from windows. Rich people had <u>slaves</u>. At night, people might have been attacked and had their money stolen. Would you want to live there?

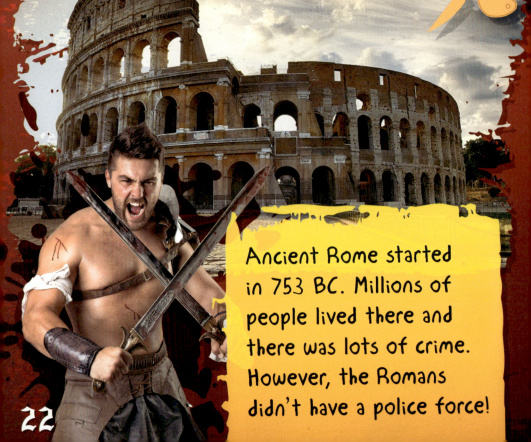

Ancient Rome started in 753 BC. Millions of people lived there and there was lots of crime. However, the Romans didn't have a police force!

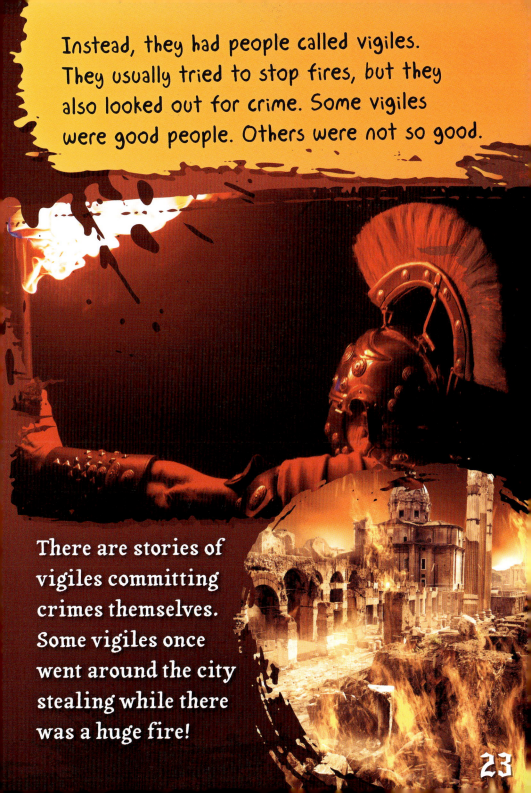

Instead, they had people called vigiles. They usually tried to stop fires, but they also looked out for crime. Some vigiles were good people. Others were not so good.

There are stories of vigiles committing crimes themselves. Some vigiles once went around the city stealing while there was a huge fire!

THE ART OF THE CON

Victor Lustig was one of the greatest conmen of all time. However, he was not always known as Victor Lustig. He had at least 47 different names.

There are no records of Victor being born at all, but we know he existed. He used words as his weapon. He was able to trick people into giving him money.

Victor once pretended to be part of the French government. He told some people who worked for metal companies that the Eiffel Tower was being sold for its metal.

He pretended to sell the Eiffel Tower to the person who offered the most money for it. When they found out it was a trick, Victor was long gone!

WITCH HUNT

Not everyone who has been found <u>guilty</u> of a crime has committed one. In the late 1600s, many people were very afraid of witches. Being a witch was a crime.

One town in the US was very afraid. It was called Salem. Three young girls said they had been cursed by three witches there. The women were thrown in prison.

ENTERING
EST. 1626
SALEM

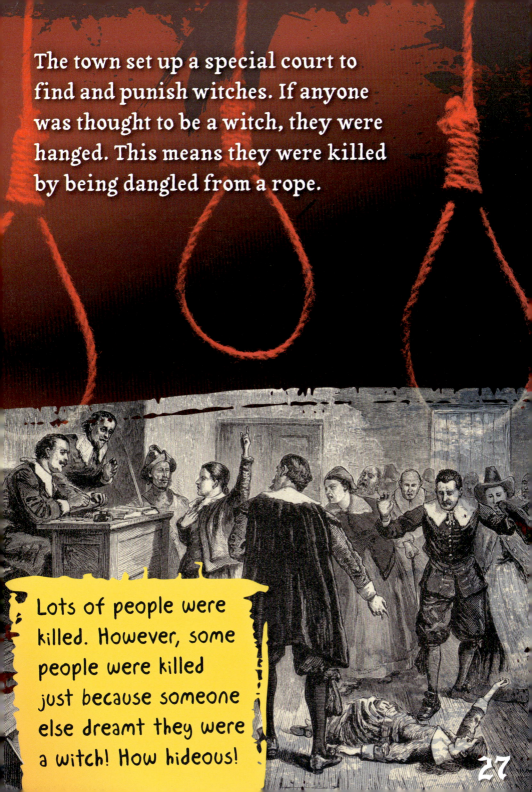

The town set up a special court to find and punish witches. If anyone was thought to be a witch, they were hanged. This means they were killed by being dangled from a rope.

Lots of people were killed. However, some people were killed just because someone else dreamt they were a witch! How hideous!

TERRIBLE TORTURE

Today, lots of different things stop people committing crimes. These include police, cameras and alarms. None of these things existed far back in the past.

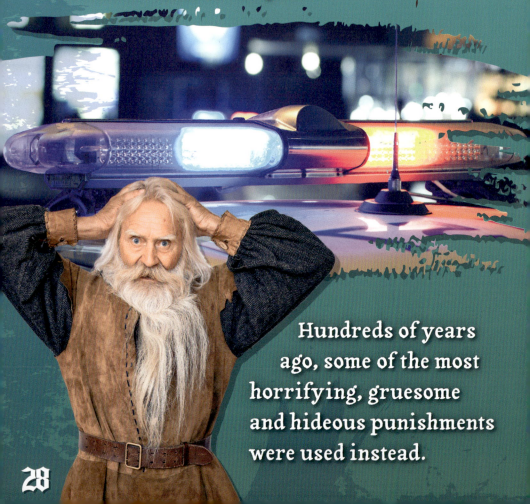

Hundreds of years ago, some of the most horrifying, gruesome and hideous punishments were used instead.

RED HOT

People might have been asked to hold a red-hot iron bar. If their hands healed after three days, they were not guilty.

CRACK THAT WHIP

People were whipped on the back if they didn't work hard enough.

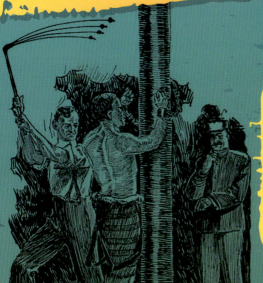

CHOP, CHOP

People were sometimes punished by having body parts cut off. Someone who was caught stealing might have had their hands chopped off.

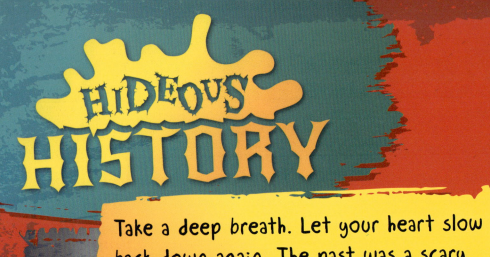

HIDEOUS HISTORY

Take a deep breath. Let your heart slow back down again. The past was a scary place to be, but you are not there now.

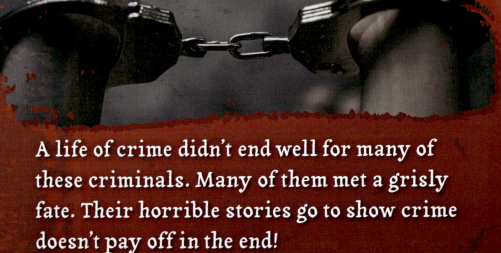

A life of crime didn't end well for many of these criminals. Many of them met a grisly fate. Their horrible stories go to show crime doesn't pay off in the end!

GLOSSARY

CENTURY a length of time that measures 100 years

GUILTY responsible for a bad action or wrongdoing

HISTORIANS people who study what happened in the past

INVESTIGATED examined facts and clues in order to find out the truth

LAW the rules people must live by

OUTLAW someone who lives a life that doesn't follow the rules people must live by

RESEARCHING finding out about a particular thing

SLAVES people who have no freedom and are owned by other people

WITNESSES people who were there at the time and promise to tell the truth about what happened

INDEX

AN INTRODUCTION TO BOOKLIFE RAPID READERS...

Packed full of gripping topics and twisted tales, BookLife Rapid Readers are perfect for older children looking to propel their reading up to top speed. With three levels based on our planet's fastest animals, children will be able to find the perfect point from which to accelerate their reading journey. From the spooky to the silly, these roaring reads will turn every child at every reading level into a prolific page-turner!

CHEETAH

The fastest animals on land, cheetahs will be taking their first strides as they race to top speed.

MARLIN

The fastest animals under water, marlins will be blasting through their journey.

FALCON

The fastest animals in the air, falcons will be flying at top speed as they tear through the skies.